MW00366493

If Lost, Please Return To:

Name:_____

Phone:_____

Email:_____

When I started counting my blessings,
my whole life turned around

-Willie Nelson

Gratitude Journal

Date: Day:

Best Moment Today:

_____
_____
_____
_____

Things I'm Grateful For Today:

1._____
2._____
3._____

Someone I'm Thankful For Today:

_____

because _____

_____

Notes:

Gratitude Journal

Date:	Day:

Best Moment Today:

_____
_____
_____
_____

Things I'm Grateful For Today:

1._____
2._____
3._____

Someone I'm Thankful For Today:

_____

because _____
_____

Notes:

Gratitude Journal

Date:	Day:

Best Moment Today:

_____

_____

_____

_____

Things I'm Grateful For Today:

1._____

2._____

3._____

Someone I'm Thankful For Today:

_____

because _____

_____

Notes:

Gratitude Journal

Date:	Day:

Best Moment Today:

_____
_____
_____
_____

Things I'm Grateful For Today:

1._____
2._____
3._____

Someone I'm Thankful For Today:

_____

because _____

_____

Notes:

Gratitude Journal

Date:	Day:

Best Moment Today:

_____
_____
_____
_____

Things I'm Grateful For Today:

1._____
2._____
3._____

Someone I'm Thankful For Today:

_____

because _____

_____

Notes:

Gratitude Journal

Date:	Day:

Best Moment Today:

_____

_____

_____

_____

Things I'm Grateful For Today:

1._____
2._____
3._____

Someone I'm Thankful For Today:

_____

because _____

_____

Notes:

Gratitude Journal

Date:	Day:

Best Moment Today:

_____
_____
_____
_____

Things I'm Grateful For Today:

1._____
2._____
3._____

Someone I'm Thankful For Today:

_____

because _____

_____

Notes:

Gratitude Journal

Date: Day:

Best Moment Today:

_____
_____
_____
_____

Things I'm Grateful For Today:

1._____
2._____
3._____

Someone I'm Thankful For Today:

_____
because _____
_____

Notes:

Gratitude Journal

Date: Day:

Best Moment Today:

_____
_____
_____
_____

Things I'm Grateful For Today:

1._____
2._____
3._____

Someone I'm Thankful For Today:

_____
because _____
_____

Notes:

Gratitude Journal

Date:	Day:

Best Moment Today:

_____
_____
_____
_____

Things I'm Grateful For Today:

1._____
2._____
3._____

Someone I'm Thankful For Today:

_____

because _____
_____

Notes:

Gratitude Journal

Date:	Day:

Best Moment Today:

_____
_____
_____
_____

Things I'm Grateful For Today:

1._____
2._____
3._____

Someone I'm Thankful For Today:

_____

because _____

_____

Notes:

Gratitude Journal

Date: Day:

Best Moment Today:

_____

_____

_____

_____

Things I'm Grateful For Today:

1._____

2._____

3._____

Someone I'm Thankful For Today:

_____

because _____

_____

Notes:

Gratitude Journal

Date: Day:

Best Moment Today:

_____
_____
_____
_____

Things I'm Grateful For Today:

1._____
2._____
3._____

Someone I'm Thankful For Today:

_____

because _____

_____

Notes:

Gratitude Journal

Date:	Day:

Best Moment Today:

_____
_____
_____
_____

Things I'm Grateful For Today:

1._____
2._____
3._____

Someone I'm Thankful For Today:

_____

because _____

_____

Notes:

Gratitude Journal

Date: Day:

Best Moment Today:

_____
_____
_____
_____

Things I'm Grateful For Today:

1._____
2._____
3._____

Someone I'm Thankful For Today:

_____

because _____

_____

Notes:

Gratitude Journal

Date:	Day:

Best Moment Today:

_____
_____
_____
_____

Things I'm Grateful For Today:

1._____
2._____
3._____

Someone I'm Thankful For Today:

_____

because _____
_____

Notes:

Gratitude Journal

Date:	Day:

Best Moment Today:

_____
_____
_____
_____

Things I'm Grateful For Today:

1._____
2._____
3._____

Someone I'm Thankful For Today:

_____

because _____

_____

Notes:

Gratitude Journal

Date: Day:

Best Moment Today:

_____
_____
_____
_____

Things I'm Grateful For Today:

1._____
2._____
3._____

Someone I'm Thankful For Today:

_____

because _____

_____

Notes:

Gratitude Journal

Date: _____ Day: _____

Best Moment Today:

_____
_____
_____
_____

Things I'm Grateful For Today:

1._____
2._____
3._____

Someone I'm Thankful For Today:

_____

because _____
_____

Notes:

Gratitude Journal

Date: Day:

Best Moment Today:

_____
_____
_____
_____

Things I'm Grateful For Today:

1._____
2._____
3._____

Someone I'm Thankful For Today:

_____

because _____

_____

Notes:

Gratitude Journal

Date:	Day:

Best Moment Today:

_____
_____
_____
_____

Things I'm Grateful For Today:

1._____
2._____
3._____

Someone I'm Thankful For Today:

_____

because _____
_____

Notes:

Gratitude Journal

Date: Day:

Best Moment Today:

_____

_____

_____

_____

Things I'm Grateful For Today:

1._____

2._____

3._____

Someone I'm Thankful For Today:

_____

because _____

_____

Notes:

Gratitude Journal

Date: **Day:**

Best Moment Today:

_____
_____
_____
_____

Things I'm Grateful For Today:

1._____
2._____
3._____

Someone I'm Thankful For Today:

_____

because _____

_____

Notes:

Gratitude Journal

Date: Day:

Best Moment Today:

_____

_____

_____

_____

Things I'm Grateful For Today:

1._____

2._____

3._____

Someone I'm Thankful For Today:

_____

because _____

_____

Notes:

Gratitude Journal

Date: _____ Day: _____

Best Moment Today:

_____

_____

_____

_____

Things I'm Grateful For Today:

1._____

2._____

3._____

Someone I'm Thankful For Today:

_____

because _____

_____

Notes:

Gratitude Journal

Date:	Day:

Best Moment Today:

_____
_____
_____
_____

Things I'm Grateful For Today:

1._____
2._____
3._____

Someone I'm Thankful For Today:

_____

because _____

_____

Notes:

Gratitude Journal

Date:	Day:

Best Moment Today:

_____
_____
_____
_____

Things I'm Grateful For Today:

1._____
2._____
3._____

Someone I'm Thankful For Today:

_____

because _____
_____

Notes:

Gratitude Journal

Date:	Day:

Best Moment Today:

_____

_____

_____

_____

Things I'm Grateful For Today:

1._____
2._____
3._____

Someone I'm Thankful For Today:

_____

because _____

_____

Notes:

Gratitude Journal

Best Moment Today:

_____
_____
_____
_____

Things I'm Grateful For Today:

1._____
2._____
3._____

Someone I'm Thankful For Today:

_____

because _____

_____

Notes:

Gratitude Journal

Date: Day:

Best Moment Today:

_____

_____

_____

_____

Things I'm Grateful For Today:

1._____

2._____

3._____

Someone I'm Thankful For Today:

_____

because _____

_____

Notes:

Gratitude Journal

Date: _____   Day: _____

Best Moment Today:

_____

_____

_____

_____

Things I'm Grateful For Today:

1._____

2._____

3._____

Someone I'm Thankful For Today:

_____

because _____

_____

Notes:

Gratitude Journal

Date: Day:

Best Moment Today:

_____

_____

_____

_____

Things I'm Grateful For Today:

1._____

2._____

3._____

Someone I'm Thankful For Today:

_____

because _____

_____

Notes:

Gratitude Journal

Date:	Day:

Best Moment Today:

_____
_____
_____
_____

Things I'm Grateful For Today:

1._____
2._____
3._____

Someone I'm Thankful For Today:

_____

because _____

_____

Notes:

Gratitude Journal

Best Moment Today:

_____
_____
_____
_____

Things I'm Grateful For Today:

1._____
2._____
3._____

Someone I'm Thankful For Today:

_____
because _____
_____

Notes:

Gratitude Journal

Best Moment Today:

_____
_____
_____
_____

Things I'm Grateful For Today:

1._____
2._____
3._____

Someone I'm Thankful For Today:

_____

because _____

_____

Notes:

Gratitude Journal

Date: Day:

Best Moment Today:

_____

_____

_____

_____

Things I'm Grateful For Today:

1._____
2._____
3._____

Someone I'm Thankful For Today:

_____

because _____

_____

Notes:

Gratitude Journal

Date: Day:

Best Moment Today:

_____
_____
_____
_____

Things I'm Grateful For Today:

1._____
2._____
3._____

Someone I'm Thankful For Today:

_____

because _____

_____

Notes:

Gratitude Journal

Date: Day:

Best Moment Today:

_____
_____
_____
_____

Things I'm Grateful For Today:

1._____
2._____
3._____

Someone I'm Thankful For Today:

_____

because _____

_____

Notes:

Gratitude Journal

Date:	Day:

Best Moment Today:

_____
_____
_____
_____

Things I'm Grateful For Today:

1._____
2._____
3._____

Someone I'm Thankful For Today:

_____

because _____

_____

Notes:

Gratitude Journal

Date:	Day:

Best Moment Today:

_____
_____
_____
_____

Things I'm Grateful For Today:

1._____
2._____
3._____

Someone I'm Thankful For Today:

_____

because _____

_____

Notes:

Gratitude Journal

Date:	Day:

Best Moment Today:

_____
_____
_____
_____

Things I'm Grateful For Today:

1._____
2._____
3._____

Someone I'm Thankful For Today:

_____

because _____
_____

Notes:

Gratitude Journal

Date: Day:

Best Moment Today:

_____
_____
_____
_____

Things I'm Grateful For Today:

1._____
2._____
3._____

Someone I'm Thankful For Today:

_____

because _____

_____

Notes:

Gratitude Journal

Date: Day:

Best Moment Today:

_____
_____
_____
_____

Things I'm Grateful For Today:

1._____
2._____
3._____

Someone I'm Thankful For Today:

_____

because _____

_____

Notes:

Gratitude Journal

Date:	Day:

Best Moment Today:

_____
_____
_____
_____

Things I'm Grateful For Today:

1._____
2._____
3._____

Someone I'm Thankful For Today:

_____

because _____
_____

Notes:

Gratitude Journal

Date:	Day:

Best Moment Today:

_____
_____
_____
_____

Things I'm Grateful For Today:

1._____
2._____
3._____

Someone I'm Thankful For Today:

_____

because _____

_____

Notes:

Gratitude Journal

Date: Day:

Best Moment Today:

_____
_____
_____
_____

Things I'm Grateful For Today:

1._____
2._____
3._____

Someone I'm Thankful For Today:

_____

because _____

_____

Notes:

Gratitude Journal

Date:	Day:

Best Moment Today:

_____
_____
_____
_____

Things I'm Grateful For Today:

1._____
2._____
3._____

Someone I'm Thankful For Today:

_____

because _____

_____

Notes:

Gratitude Journal

Date:	Day:

Best Moment Today:

_____
_____
_____
_____

Things I'm Grateful For Today:

1._____
2._____
3._____

Someone I'm Thankful For Today:

_____

because _____

_____

Notes:

Gratitude Journal

Date:	Day:

Best Moment Today:

_____
_____
_____
_____

Things I'm Grateful For Today:

1._____
2._____
3._____

Someone I'm Thankful For Today:

_____

because _____

_____

Notes:

Gratitude Journal

Date:	Day:

Best Moment Today:

_____
_____
_____
_____

Things I'm Grateful For Today:

1._____
2._____
3._____

Someone I'm Thankful For Today:

_____

because _____

_____

Notes:

Gratitude Journal

Date: Day:

Best Moment Today:

_____

_____

_____

_____

Things I'm Grateful For Today:

1._____

2._____

3._____

Someone I'm Thankful For Today:

_____

because _____

_____

Notes:

Gratitude Journal

Date: _____   Day: _____

Best Moment Today:

_____
_____
_____
_____

Things I'm Grateful For Today:

1._____
2._____
3._____

Someone I'm Thankful For Today:

_____

because _____

_____

Notes:

Gratitude Journal

Date:	Day:

Best Moment Today:

_____
_____
_____
_____

Things I'm Grateful For Today:

1._____
2._____
3._____

Someone I'm Thankful For Today:

_____

because _____

_____

Notes:

Gratitude Journal

Date: Day:

Best Moment Today:

_____
_____
_____
_____

Things I'm Grateful For Today:

1._____
2._____
3._____

Someone I'm Thankful For Today:

_____
because _____
_____

Notes:

Gratitude Journal

Date: Day:

Best Moment Today:

_____

_____

_____

_____

Things I'm Grateful For Today:

1._____

2._____

3._____

Someone I'm Thankful For Today:

_____

because _____

_____

Notes:

Gratitude Journal

Date: Day:

Best Moment Today:

_____

_____

_____

_____

Things I'm Grateful For Today:

1._____

2._____

3._____

Someone I'm Thankful For Today:

_____

because _____

_____

Notes:

Gratitude Journal

Date:	Day:

Best Moment Today:

_____
_____
_____
_____

Things I'm Grateful For Today:

1._____
2._____
3._____

Someone I'm Thankful For Today:

_____

because _____

_____

Notes:

Gratitude Journal

Date: Day:

Best Moment Today:

_____

_____

_____

_____

Things I'm Grateful For Today:

1._____

2._____

3._____

Someone I'm Thankful For Today:

_____

because _____

_____

Notes:

Gratitude Journal

Date:	Day:

Best Moment Today:

_____
_____
_____
_____

Things I'm Grateful For Today:

1._____
2._____
3._____

Someone I'm Thankful For Today:

_____

because _____

_____

Notes:

Gratitude Journal

Date:	Day:

Best Moment Today:

_____
_____
_____
_____

Things I'm Grateful For Today:

1._____
2._____
3._____

Someone I'm Thankful For Today:

_____
because _____
_____

Notes:

Gratitude Journal

Date:	Day:

Best Moment Today:

_____
_____
_____
_____

Things I'm Grateful For Today:

1._____
2._____
3._____

Someone I'm Thankful For Today:

_____

because _____
_____

Notes:

Gratitude Journal

Date:	Day:

Best Moment Today:

_____
_____
_____
_____

Things I'm Grateful For Today:

1._____
2._____
3._____

Someone I'm Thankful For Today:

_____

because _____

_____

Notes:

Gratitude Journal

Date: Day:

Best Moment Today:

_____
_____
_____
_____

Things I'm Grateful For Today:

1._____
2._____
3._____

Someone I'm Thankful For Today:

_____

because _____

_____

Notes:

Gratitude Journal

Date:	Day:

Best Moment Today:

_____
_____
_____
_____

Things I'm Grateful For Today:

1._____
2._____
3._____

Someone I'm Thankful For Today:

_____

because _____

_____

Notes:

Gratitude Journal

Date:	Day:

Best Moment Today:

_____

_____

_____

_____

Things I'm Grateful For Today:

1._____

2._____

3._____

Someone I'm Thankful For Today:

_____

because _____

_____

Notes:

Gratitude Journal

Date:	Day:

Best Moment Today:

_____
_____
_____
_____

Things I'm Grateful For Today:

1._____
2._____
3._____

Someone I'm Thankful For Today:

_____

because _____

_____

Notes:

Gratitude Journal

Date: _____ Day: _____

Best Moment Today:

_____

_____

_____

_____

Things I'm Grateful For Today:

1. _____

2. _____

3. _____

Someone I'm Thankful For Today:

_____

because _____

_____

Notes:

Gratitude Journal

Date:	Day:

Best Moment Today:

_____
_____
_____
_____

Things I'm Grateful For Today:

1._____
2._____
3._____

Someone I'm Thankful For Today:

_____

because _____

_____

Notes:

Gratitude Journal

Date: Day:

Best Moment Today:

_____

_____

_____

_____

Things I'm Grateful For Today:

1._____

2._____

3._____

Someone I'm Thankful For Today:

_____

because _____

_____

Notes:

Gratitude Journal

Date:	Day:

Best Moment Today:

_____
_____
_____
_____

Things I'm Grateful For Today:

1._____
2._____
3._____

Someone I'm Thankful For Today:

_____

because _____
_____

Notes:

Gratitude Journal

Date: Day:

Best Moment Today:

_____
_____
_____
_____

Things I'm Grateful For Today:

1._____
2._____
3._____

Someone I'm Thankful For Today:

_____

because _____

_____

Notes:

Gratitude Journal

Date:	Day:

Best Moment Today:

_____

_____

_____

_____

Things I'm Grateful For Today:

1._____

2._____

3._____

Someone I'm Thankful For Today:

_____

because _____

_____

Notes:

Gratitude Journal

Date: Day:

Best Moment Today:

_____
_____
_____
_____

Things I'm Grateful For Today:

1._____
2._____
3._____

Someone I'm Thankful For Today:

_____

because _____

_____

Notes:

Gratitude Journal

Date: Day:

Best Moment Today:

_____

_____

_____

_____

Things I'm Grateful For Today:

1._____

2._____

3._____

Someone I'm Thankful For Today:

_____

because _____

_____

Notes:

Gratitude Journal

Date: Day:

Best Moment Today:

_____
_____
_____
_____

Things I'm Grateful For Today:

1._____
2._____
3._____

Someone I'm Thankful For Today:

_____
because _____
_____

Notes:

Gratitude Journal

Date:	Day:

Best Moment Today:

_____
_____
_____
_____

Things I'm Grateful For Today:

1._____
2._____
3._____

Someone I'm Thankful For Today:

_____

because _____

_____

Notes:

Gratitude Journal

Date: Day:

Best Moment Today:

_____
_____
_____
_____

Things I'm Grateful For Today:

1._____
2._____
3._____

Someone I'm Thankful For Today:

_____

because _____

_____

Notes:

Gratitude Journal

Date: Day:

Best Moment Today:

_____

_____

_____

_____

Things I'm Grateful For Today:

1._____

2._____

3._____

Someone I'm Thankful For Today:

_____

because _____

_____

Notes:

Gratitude Journal

Date: Day:

Best Moment Today:

_____
_____
_____
_____

Things I'm Grateful For Today:

1._____
2._____
3._____

Someone I'm Thankful For Today:

_____

because _____
_____

Notes:

Gratitude Journal

Date: Day:

Best Moment Today:

_____
_____
_____
_____

Things I'm Grateful For Today:

1._____
2._____
3._____

Someone I'm Thankful For Today:

_____

because _____

_____

Notes:

Gratitude Journal

Date: Day:

Best Moment Today:

_____
_____
_____
_____

Things I'm Grateful For Today:

1._____
2._____
3._____

Someone I'm Thankful For Today:

_____

because _____

_____

Notes:

Gratitude Journal

Date: _____ Day: _____

Best Moment Today:

_____

_____

_____

_____

Things I'm Grateful For Today:

1._____

2._____

3._____

Someone I'm Thankful For Today:

_____

because _____

_____

Notes:

Gratitude Journal

Date:	Day:

Best Moment Today:

_____
_____
_____
_____

Things I'm Grateful For Today:

1._____
2._____
3._____

Someone I'm Thankful For Today:

_____

because _____

_____

Notes:

Gratitude Journal

Date:	Day:

Best Moment Today:

_____
_____
_____
_____

Things I'm Grateful For Today:

1._____
2._____
3._____

Someone I'm Thankful For Today:

_____

because _____

_____

Notes:

Gratitude Journal

Date:	Day:

Best Moment Today:

_____
_____
_____
_____

Things I'm Grateful For Today:

1._____
2._____
3._____

Someone I'm Thankful For Today:

_____

because _____
_____

Notes:

Gratitude Journal

Date: Day:

Best Moment Today:

_____
_____
_____
_____

Things I'm Grateful For Today:

1._____
2._____
3._____

Someone I'm Thankful For Today:

_____

because _____

_____

Notes:

Gratitude Journal

Date:	Day:

Best Moment Today:

_____
_____
_____
_____

Things I'm Grateful For Today:

1._____
2._____
3._____

Someone I'm Thankful For Today:

_____

because _____

_____

Notes:

Gratitude Journal

Date: Day:

Best Moment Today:

_____
_____
_____
_____

Things I'm Grateful For Today:

1._____
2._____
3._____

Someone I'm Thankful For Today:

_____
because _____
_____

Notes:

Gratitude Journal

Date: Day:

Best Moment Today:

_____

_____

_____

_____

Things I'm Grateful For Today:

1._____

2._____

3._____

Someone I'm Thankful For Today:

_____

because _____

_____

Notes:

Gratitude Journal

Date:	Day:

Best Moment Today:

_____
_____
_____
_____

Things I'm Grateful For Today:

1._____
2._____
3._____

Someone I'm Thankful For Today:

_____

because _____

_____

Notes:

Gratitude Journal

Date: _____ Day: _____

Best Moment Today:

_____
_____
_____
_____

Things I'm Grateful For Today:

1._____
2._____
3._____

Someone I'm Thankful For Today:

_____

because _____

_____

Notes:

Gratitude Journal

Date: Day:

Best Moment Today:

_____

_____

_____

_____

Things I'm Grateful For Today:

1._____

2._____

3._____

Someone I'm Thankful For Today:

_____

because _____

_____

Notes:

Gratitude Journal

Date:	Day:

Best Moment Today:

_____
_____
_____
_____

Things I'm Grateful For Today:

1._____
2._____
3._____

Someone I'm Thankful For Today:

_____

because _____

_____

Notes:

Gratitude Journal

Date: Day:

Best Moment Today:

_____

_____

_____

_____

Things I'm Grateful For Today:

1._____

2._____

3._____

Someone I'm Thankful For Today:

_____

because _____

_____

Notes:

Gratitude Journal

Date: Day:

Best Moment Today:

_____
_____
_____
_____

Things I'm Grateful For Today:

1._____
2._____
3._____

Someone I'm Thankful For Today:

_____

because _____

_____

Notes:

Gratitude Journal

Date:	Day:

Best Moment Today:

_____
_____
_____
_____

Things I'm Grateful For Today:

1._____
2._____
3._____

Someone I'm Thankful For Today:

_____

because _____

_____

Notes:

Gratitude Journal

Date: Day:

Best Moment Today:

_____
_____
_____
_____

Things I'm Grateful For Today:

1._____
2._____
3._____

Someone I'm Thankful For Today:

_____
because _____
_____

Notes:

Gratitude Journal

Date:	Day:

Best Moment Today:

_____
_____
_____
_____

Things I'm Grateful For Today:

1._____
2._____
3._____

Someone I'm Thankful For Today:

_____

because _____
_____

Notes:

Gratitude Journal

Date: Day:

Best Moment Today:

_____
_____
_____
_____

Things I'm Grateful For Today:

1._____
2._____
3._____

Someone I'm Thankful For Today:

_____

because _____

_____

Notes:

Gratitude Journal

Date:	Day:

Best Moment Today:

_____
_____
_____
_____

Things I'm Grateful For Today:

1._____
2._____
3._____

Someone I'm Thankful For Today:

_____

because _____

_____

Notes:

Made in the USA
Monee, IL
17 January 2023

25454261R00059